ECOLOGICAL DISASTERS

by Barbara M. Linde

Table of Contents

Pictures To Think About

Words To Think About

Characteristics

poisonous

harmful to people

?

toxic

What do you think the word **toxic** means?

Examples

chemicals

waste

?

pesticide

What do you think the word **pesticide** means?

English:
pest
(rodent or insect)

Latin:
cide
(to kill)

Read for More Clues
ecological
disaster,   page 2
pesticide,   page 10
toxic,   page 10

ecological disaster

What do you think the words **ecological disaster** mean?

What is an ecological disaster?

| oil spill | ? | chemical leak |

What causes an ecological disaster?

| accident | ? | bad equipment |

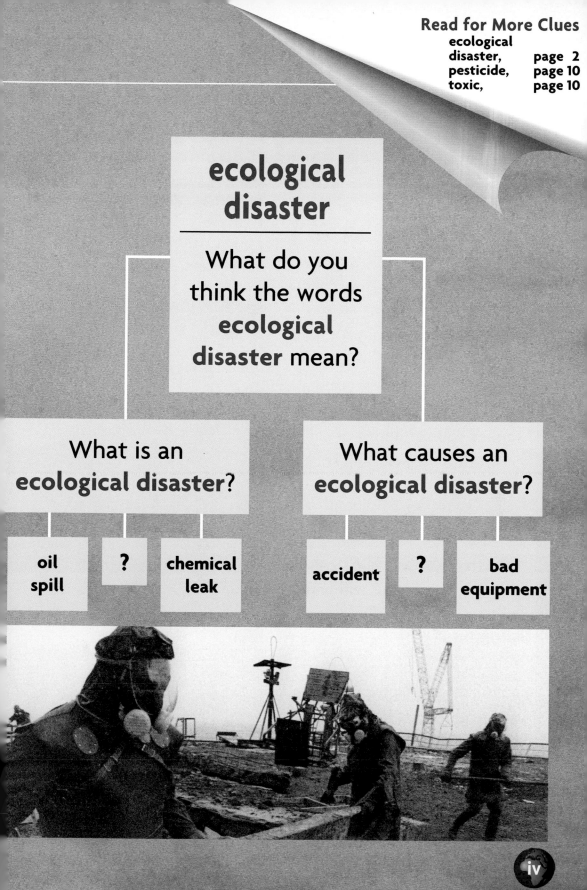

iv

Introduction

A wildfire burns out of control. The fire wipes out a whole town. A tank in a chemical factory leaks. Thousands of people are killed. Part of a nuclear power plant explodes. The area around the plant is destroyed. An oil tanker spills millions of gallons of oil into the sea. The sticky black oil kills many animals.

In this book, you will read about these **ecological disasters** (eh-kuh-LAH-jih-kul dih-ZAS-terz). You will learn how each one hurt people, wildlife, and the environment. You will find out why these awful things happened. Then you will learn what is being done now.

▲ A huge oil spill killed a large number of wildlife in Prince William Sound, Alaska.

The Great Peshtigo Fire

O n October 8, 1871, the night sky turned red over the town of Peshtigo (PESH-tih-go). Thick, dark smoke filled the air. A wall of fire was moving toward the town!

Terrified townspeople ran for the river. Balls of fire hit the people as they ran. The town was destroyed.

What caused the fire? The land and forests were dry. No snow or rain had fallen for months.

Peshtigo was a growing town. Farmers and loggers had cut down and burned trees. They didn't put out all the fires. Railroad workers laid track for new lines. They left piles of branches along the sides of the tracks. Sometimes sparks from trains set the dry branches on fire.

▲ The Great Peshtigo Fire of 1871 is still the worst forest fire in U.S. history.

EYEWITNESS ACCOUNT

The *Marinette and Peshtigo Eagle* newspaper printed the first report of the fire the following day.

"The streets were lined with men, women and children fleeing for their lives. Many of the families were engaged in making excavations in the sand and burying their household goods. Any quantity of goods was hauled over onto the Island. The sick were being removed to places of safety, and thus, with alternate hope and despair, the long, weary hours of the night wore away."

CHAPTER 1

A Tornado Hits

Small fires had been burning in the forest around Peshtigo for weeks. Many fires had been put out, but some still burned. Then a huge **tornado** (tor-NAY-doh) sprang up on the night of October 8. The fierce winds turned the small fires into a huge firestorm. The fire was as wide as several football fields.

In only five minutes, the entire town was on fire. Some people ran for safety in the Peshtigo River. An hour later, the town was gone.

The next day, the winds died down. Rain began to fall. The rain put out the fire. The fire had destroyed millions of dollars' worth of property. Between 1,500 and 2,400 people died.

In a few years, people rebuilt Peshtigo. Soon, crops and forests were growing again. Today the town has a museum to remember the fire and its victims.

▲ During the Peshtigo fire, many people spent several terrifying hours in the river.

▲ Three hundred people died in the Great Chicago Fire.

The Great Chicago Fire

On the same night as the Great Peshtigo Fire, another fire blazed through the city of Chicago, Illinois, 250 miles (402 kilometers) south of Peshtigo. It is said that the fire started in a barn that belonged to Mr. and Mrs. O'Leary. Flames whipped through the city for about twenty-four hours. Three hundred people died and 90,000 lost their homes. The fire caused $200 million in damages.

Could Peshtigo Have Been Prevented?

Weather was one cause of the fire. No one can control the weather. So, the answer is no. The fire probably could not have been prevented.

Still, the fire could have been controlled better. Long ago, people did not know much about controlling fires. Also, Peshtigo had only one fire engine! A horse pulled the engine slowly.

What Is Being Done Now?

Another large forest fire burned in Idaho in 1910. After that, the government started the National Parks System. This system protects our forests.

In 1944, the United States Forest Service made posters. The posters had a cartoon bear named Smokey. Smokey gave tips on preventing forest fires. He still does today.

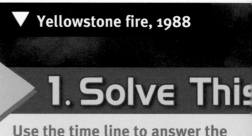

▼ **Yellowstone fire, 1988**

1. Solve This

Use the time line to answer the following questions.

a. List the fires in order from great to least number of acres burned.

b. Which fires burned more acres than the Great Peshtigo Fire? How many more acres?

Great Peshtigo Fire	Great Idaho Fire
Wisconsin and Michigan	**Idaho and Montana**
1871	**1910**
1,500,000 acres	3,000,000 acres

Today we know a lot more about preventing and controlling fires. Forest fires still happen, but they can be controlled. Rangers check parks often for fires.

Firefighters put out fires quickly. They use airplanes and chemicals to fight fires.

Math ✓ Point

Which type of graph would you choose to display this data?

...llowstone Fire ...ontana and Idaho	Inowak Fire Alaska	Cerro Grande New Mexico	Rumsey Fire California
1988	**1997**	**2000**	**2004**
585,000 acres	610,000 acres	47,650 acres	39,138 acres

The Bhopal Chemical Spill

Bhopal (BOH-pahl) is a city in India. During the night of December 2, 1984, the people of Bhopal were sleeping. In a nearby chemical (KEH-mih-kul) factory, a pipe started to leak. Then gas began to spray from the tank.

The workers were scared. The workers did not know what to do. Many ran away. Huge clouds of gas spread into the air. The gas filled the town.

People in Bhopal woke up coughing. The people's lungs burned. Their eyes stung. More than two thousand people died that day.

What did the chemical factory make? The Union Carbide factory in Bhopal made **pesticides** (PES-tih-sides). Pesticides are chemicals that kill insects. One pesticide is MIC. This chemical is **toxic** (TAHK-sik), or very harmful.

▲ Hundreds of thousands of people fled Bhopal in the days following the accident.

▲ the Union Carbide chemical plant

▲ **The poison gas blinded thousands of people.**

What Happened?

The MIC was in a large tank in the factory. The tank often leaked small amounts. Workers were not alarmed. But workers did not know that water had gotten into the tank.

The water mixed with the MIC. This made a very toxic gas. The safety vent was not working. Workers realized what was happening, but it was too late. The gas was spreading over the city.

None of the workers were hurt. The workers were trained to run away from the wind. Local people were not trained. They did not know what to do.

Some people ran right into the cloud of gas. People became very sick. Many people were blinded. They did not know to put wet towels over their faces. This would have protected their eyes.

2. Solve This

Approximately 40 tons of gas leaked that night in Bhopal. Union Carbide claimed that about 4,000 people died as a result, though other reports said it was 8,000 in the first week alone. An estimated 150,000 to 600,000 people were injured. At least 15,000 died from their injuries. Using the greater estimate, what percentage of the injured survived?

EYEWITNESS ACCOUNT

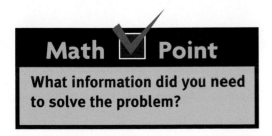

" At about 12:30 A.M. I woke up to the sound of my baby coughing badly. In the half light I saw that the room was filled with a white cloud. I heard a lot of people shouting. They were shouting 'run, run.' Then I started coughing with each breath seeming as if I was breathing in fire. My eyes were burning."

—Aziza Sultan, survivor of the Bhopal spill

Math ✓ Point

What information did you need to solve the problem?

Could the Spill Have Been Prevented?

A report said that the spill was caused by workers' mistakes and bad equipment. The answer is yes. The spill could have been prevented.

The Union Carbide Company paid $470 million to the victims. The spill has still not been completely cleaned up. People from 179 villages are still at risk of getting sick or dying. People are asking the company and the Indian government to finish the cleanup.

▲ Protesters wanted to put the head of Union Carbide on trial for not doing enough to help the victims of the Bhopal disaster.

What Is Being Done Now?

People took action after the spill. New rules make sure that:

- Chemical companies are regularly checked for safety.
- Workers store chemicals more carefully.
- Workers know how to use the equipment.
- Workers know what to do in case of an accident.
- Workers know how to clean up accidents safely and quickly.

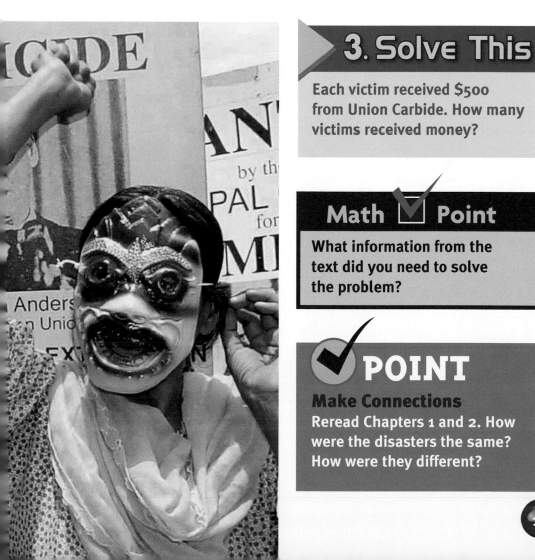

3. Solve This

Each victim received $500 from Union Carbide. How many victims received money?

Math ☑ Point

What information from the text did you need to solve the problem?

✓ POINT

Make Connections
Reread Chapters 1 and 2. How were the disasters the same? How were they different?

The Chernobyl Disaster

The time was 11 p.m. on April 25, 1986. Workers at a **nuclear** (NOO-klee-er) power plant in Ukraine (YOO-krayne) began a test.

The workers were testing a **reactor** (ree-AK-ter). A reactor splits atoms without causing an explosion. The test did not go as planned.

▲ The Chernobyl-4 reactor before the explosion . . .

Explosion!

At about 1:23 a.m. on April 26, two explosions rocked the reactor. Workers did not know how bad the explosions were. Many people lived outside the city of Chernobyl (CHER-noh-bul). Their lives would never be the same.

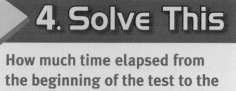

4. Solve This

How much time elapsed from the beginning of the test to the moment when the explosion happened?

Math ✓ Point

What strategy did you use to solve the problem?

▲ . . . and after the explosion.

▲ After the explosion, workers wore protective gear while they checked radiation levels. The aprons were made of lead. The overalls were made of rubber and lead.

What Happened?

During the test, the splitting atoms got too hot. Water in the reactor turned into too much steam. The steam blew the lid off the reactor.

A shield kept the **radioactive** (ray-dee-oh-AK-tiv) materials in the reactor. The shield blew off. Burning radioactive material burst out.

A huge radioactive cloud formed. Fires started to burn. Brave people fought the fires and saved the power plant.

No one realized how much radioactive material they were breathing in. The material was in the air and on people's skin.

EYEWITNESS ACCOUNT

Nuclear power plant worker Sasha Yuvchenko was at Chernobyl the night it exploded.

"There was a heavy thud. A couple of seconds later, I felt a wave come through the room. The thick concrete walls were bent like rubber . . . . Steam wrapped around everything; it was dark and there was a horrible hissing noise. There was no ceiling, only sky—a sky full of stars."

5. Solve This

The green area on the map shows the contamination cloud on May 12, 1986. What is the greatest distance it spread from the Chernobyl reactor? Write your answer to the nearest hundred miles.

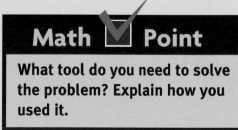

Math ☑ Point

What tool do you need to solve the problem? Explain how you used it.

Later, many of the firefighters and workers died or became very sick. The land and water became toxic.

Villages as far as 20 miles (32 kilometers) away were poisoned. More than 135,000 people had to leave their homes.

CHAPTER 3

Could Chernobyl Have Been Prevented?

Some people say that the workers were not well trained. Maybe with better training the workers could have prevented the accident. Other people say that the nuclear reactor was not well designed. Maybe with a better design the reactor would not have exploded.

We may never know if this disaster could have been prevented. We do know that failed equipment and human error both played a role.

▲ This photograph taken years after the Chernobyl-4 accident shows an eerily empty amusement park.

What Is Being Done Now?

Today the world knows how dangerous nuclear power can be. Nuclear power plants are more carefully designed. The plants have better safety features in place.

Safer systems are now used in nuclear power plants. Workers in power plants get better training. People who live nearby have also been taught what to do in an emergency.

EYEWITNESS ACCOUNT

In 2004, a Russian photographer named Elena Filatova traveled to the site of the Chernobyl-4 accident. She took pictures of the abandoned town and wrote down how she felt about what she saw.

"At first glance, the ghost town seems like a normal town. There is a taxi stop, a grocery store, someone's wash hanging from the balcony and the windows are open . . . Then I realize those were opened in the spring of April, 1986 . . . Now there are places here where no one dares to go, not even scientists with protective gear."

▲ On December 15, 2000, the entire Chernobyl Nuclear Power Station closed down for good.

21

The *Exxon Valdez* Oil Spill

It was near midnight on March 24, 1989. The *Exxon Valdez* moved quietly over the sea in Alaska. This huge oil tanker carried fifty-three million gallons of oil.

The third mate was steering the ship. He saw blocks of ice ahead. He tried to turn the ship to miss the ice. He did not see the reef below the ship. A reef is a ridge of rock under the surface of the ocean.

Suddenly the tanker's hull, or bottom, scraped against the reef. Sharp rocks tore open the ship. With a jolt, the ship came to a stop. Oil began to gush out. The thick, black oil filled the water. Soon, the beaches and wildlife were covered with oil.

▲ The *Exxon Valdez* tanker is aground on Bligh Reef. Another ship is taking off the remaining oil.

IT'S A FACT

The *Exxon Valdez* was longer than three football fields. Its depth in the water was the same as a five-story building.

6. Solve This

A ship's speed is measured in knots. One knot is equal to 1.15 miles per hour. The *Exxon Valdez* was traveling at 12 knots when it hit Bligh Reef. What was the speed in miles per hour?

Math ☑ Point

What operation did you use to solve the problem?

An Ecological Nightmare

Rocks tore holes in eight of the ship's eleven oil tanks. More than five million gallons of oil came out in the first three hours.

The only way to get to the spill site was by boat or helicopter. Help came twelve hours after the ship crashed. By that time, about eleven million gallons of oil had spilled into the water.

Thousands of birds and sea otters died within hours. The oil stuck to their feathers or fur. Cold air reached the animals' skin. The animals died from the cold. Some birds and otters tried to clean the oil off. They swallowed the oil. The oil poisoned them.

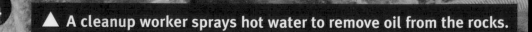

▲ A cleanup worker sprays hot water to remove oil from the rocks.

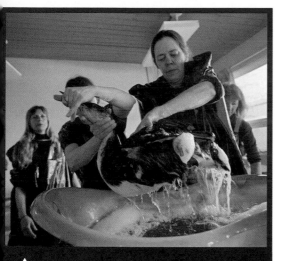

▲ Workers cleaned many birds like this one.

Math ✓ Point

Use data from the table to create a different problem. Write the problem and solution.

7. Solve This

Estimated Loss of Wildlife

Type of Wildlife	Number Lost
Sea birds	250,000
Sea otters	2,800
Harbor seals	300
Bald eagles	250
Killer whales	22
Salmon and herring eggs	billions

Use the table to answer the following questions. Your answers will be estimates.

a. About 1,000 times as many sea birds were killed as what other type of wildlife?

b. About 10,000 times as many sea birds were killed as what other type of wildlife?

Animal Rescue

Many people worked to save the sea otters. Workers washed off the oil. Then they put the otters in warm water. Scientists gave the otters medicine to keep them from getting sick. Only 50 of the 348 otters treated lived. Still, scientists learned more about how to care for otters after an oil spill.

25

The oil spill also poisoned the sea. Many fish were coated with oil and died. Fish eggs were coated with oil. The eggs could not hatch. Many animals that eat fish starved.

Native Americans live nearby. These people get most of their food from the sea. After the spill, their food was no longer safe to eat. People had to travel long distances to buy food.

Cleanup

Cleaning up the spill took years. The United States Coast Guard helped. Volunteers from all over the world came to help.

The oil company also worked to clean up the beaches and the sea. The company paid billions of dollars for the cleanup. Today, there is still some oil below the beaches.

Some good things happened as a result of the spill. A lot of land in the area is now protected. This means there are safe places for the animals.

▲ **This machine blasts oil-coated rocks to clean them.**

8. Solve This

The *Exxon Valdez* spilled about 10.8 million gallons of oil. That's enough to fill 125 Olympic-sized swimming pools. Exxon spent 2.5 billion dollars for cleanup. In addition, Exxon spent about 1 billion dollars in court settlements. The company was sued for about 5 billion dollars for damage to natural resources and other damage. About how much did Exxon spend as a result of the accident?

Math ✔ Point

What information was necessary to solve the problem? Which information was not needed?

Many visitors come to see how well the area has recovered.

Could the *Exxon Valdez* Oil Spill Have Been Prevented?

People studied the accident to find out what had happened. They decided that it took place because of human error. The answer is yes. The accident could have been prevented.

What Is Being Done Now?

Oil tankers are safer now. Here is why:

- The U.S. Coast Guard checks tankers for safety.
- Each tanker has a written plan for cleaning up an oil spill.
- By 2015, all tankers must have double hulls. This will make these ships stronger.
- Tankers have cleanup materials ready to use.

Modern Disasters

1871	1984
Peshtigo Fire	Bhopal Chemical Spill

Conclusion

This book has told about some terrible ecological disasters. Places were destroyed. People and wildlife were hurt or killed. Human error, events in nature, and bad equipment were some of the causes.

How can we stop disasters like these from happening in the future? Companies need to train their workers. They must make sure their equipment is safe. Lastly, we must have rules and laws that help keep people, wildlife, and places safe.

POINT

Think About It
Which ecological disaster do you think was the worst? Why?

1986

Chernobyl Disaster

1989

Exxon Valdez **Oil Spill**

29

Solve This Answers

1. Page 8
a. Fires in order of greatest to least number of acres burned are: Great Idaho Fire, Yellowstone Fire, Great Peshtigo Fire, Inowak Fire, Cerro Grande Fire, Rumsey Fire.
b. The Great Idaho Fire burned 1,500,000 more acres and the Yellowstone Fire burned 85,000 more acres.

Math Checkpoint. A bar graph would allow you to compare data at a glance.

2. Page 13
97.5%

Math Checkpoint. Needed information is the greater estimate of the injured (600,000) and number of injured who died (15,000). Divide 15,000 by 600,000 = .025 or 2.5%. Subtract 2.5% from 100% to get 97.5%.

3. Page 15
940,000 victims. $470,000,000 divided by $500 per victim = 940,000 victims.

Math Checkpoint. Information from text needed: the total amount of money paid out, $470 million.

4. Page 17
2 hours and 23 minutes

Math Checkpoint. A clock would be used to count the hours between 11 and 1, then add the 23 minutes.

5. Page 19
Approximately 1,100 miles

Math Checkpoint. A ruler is needed. Measure the distance from the reactor to the farthest edge of the cloud (1.75 inches), then use the map scale. 0.5 inches represents 300 miles.

6. Page 23
13.8 miles per hour

Math Checkpoint. Multiplication should be used. 1.15 knots per mile x 12 knots per hour = 13.8 miles per hour.

7. Page 25
a. About 1,000 times as many sea birds were killed as bald eagles.
b. About 10,000 times as many sea birds were killed as killer whales.

Math Checkpoint. Answers will vary. Possible response: What was the total loss of wildlife, excluding salmon and herring eggs, caused by the *Exxon Valdez* spill? About 253,372 animals lost.

8. Page 27
$3.5 billion

Math Checkpoint. $2.5 billion spent on cleanup and $1 billion spent on court settlements. Information not needed: amount of oil spilled, and amount company was sued for.

Glossary

ecological
disaster
(eh-kuh-LAH-jih-kul dih-ZAS-ter) an event that has a harmful effect on the environment (page 2)

nuclear
(NOO-klee-er) relates to the energy produced by splitting the nucleus of an atom (page 16)

pesticide
(PES-tih-side) a chemical used to kill insects (page 10)

radioactive
(ray-dee-oh-AK-tiv) giving off dangerous energy waves (page 18)

reactor
(ree-AK-ter) equipment made to start and control a nuclear reaction (page 16)

tornado
(tor-NAY-doh) a weather phenomenon characterized by strong winds that blow in a circle and cause damage to land and property (page 6)

toxic
(TAHK-sik) harmful to life or health (page 10)

Index